Pressed... But Not Destroyed

A Memoir of Exhaustion, Surrender, and Becoming

Published by Watkins Publishing Group

ISBN: 979-8-9959925-0-9 (Paperback) ISBN: 979-8-9959925-1-6 (eBook)

Printed in the United States of America

First Edition, 2026

Unless otherwise noted, all Scripture quotations are taken from the King James Version (KJV) of the Bible. Public domain.

This memoir reflects the author's present recollections of experiences over time.

Dedication

To the woman who kept going... even when she was tired.

To the one who carried more than she ever spoke about. Who showed up for everyone else... while quietly losing herself.

This is for you.

To the version of you that kept showing up even when she had nothing left. She was brave. And to the version of you that is learning to rest. She is becoming something remarkable.

May you find the strength to release what was never yours to carry. May you rediscover who you are beneath the pressure. And may you walk in a peace that no longer requires you to perform.

You were never meant to break. You were meant to become.

Author's Note

This book was not written from a place of perfection. It was written from a place of process.

There was a time when I thought strength meant holding everything together. Showing up no matter what. Carrying what needed to be carried. Pushing through, even when I was exhausted. From the outside, it looked like I had it all together. But internally, I was overwhelmed.

This journey, Pressed... But Not Destroyed was born out of that space. Not just the breaking, but the becoming that followed. Not just the pressure, but the purpose it revealed.

These pages are a reflection of real moments quiet ones, hard ones, and honest ones. Moments where I had to face myself, release what was never mine, and learn how to live in alignment instead of survival.

If you see yourself anywhere in these chapters. In the exhaustion, in the over-carrying, in the silent battles know this: you are not alone. And more importantly, you are not being destroyed by what you're going through. You are being refined.

I didn't write this book as someone who has arrived. I wrote it as someone who is still becoming. And I think that matters. Because too often we wait until everything is fully resolved before we share what we've been through. But there is something powerful about speaking from the middle of the journey from the place where the breaking has happened but the building is still underway. These pages were written from that place. Honest. Unpolished. Real. And I pray that honesty gives you permission to be honest too.

My prayer is that as you read this book, you don't just understand the words, you feel them. That you give yourself permission to pause, to reflect, and to release what no longer belongs to you. And that somewhere along the way, you begin to experience what I did:

Peace that doesn't come from everything being perfect... but from finally being aligned.

Acknowledgments

First, I give honor and gratitude to my Lord and Savior, Jesus Christ.

For His grace in the quiet moments. For His presence when I didn't have the words. For holding me steady when I felt uncertain, and for reminding me that even in silence He was still there. This book would not exist without that covering.

To every experience that stretched me, every moment that forced me to pause, and every season that required me to grow, thank you. Even when I didn't understand it, it was shaping me into who I am today.

To those who have shown me love, support, and grace whether through presence, encouragement, or simply allowing me the space to grow I am deeply grateful.

And to every reader, thank you for allowing my story to meet you where you are.

Whether you found this book in a season of exhaustion, confusion, or quiet searching I believe it found you for a reason. Not by accident. But by design. Because God has a way of placing the right words in front of us at exactly the right moment. And I pray these words were that for you.

My hope is that these words remind you of something you may have forgotten:

You are allowed to rest. You are allowed to choose yourself. And you are allowed to grow beyond what once defined you.

With gratitude to my church family at Faith Tabernacle of Prayer for all People for your leadership, love, support, and covering.

Table of Contents

FRONT MATTER

Part One — The Weight

Part Two — The Breaking

Part Three — The Healing

Part Four — The Becoming

Part Five — The Victory

BACK MATTER

Part One

The Weight

Chapter 1

The Woman Who Looked Fine

I remember sitting in my car one Saturday, engine off, hands resting on the steering wheel...completely still. The day had just ended. Everything went the way it was supposed to. I showed up. I smiled. I led. I gave. Just like I always did. And yet...I couldn't move. Not because I was busy. Not because I was distracted. But because I had nothing left in me to give. That was the moment I realized something I hadn't been ready to admit: I wasn't just tired. I was empty. And the version of me everyone thought was "strong" was quietly running on nothing.

If you had asked anyone how I was doing, they would've said the same thing: she's good, she's strong, she always has it together. And the truth is, I made sure it looked that way.

I knew how to show up. I knew how to smile at the right moments, say the right things, carry conversations, handle responsibilities, and meet expectations. I knew how to be dependable. I knew how to be present. I knew how to be everything people needed me to be. And for a long time, I wore that like a badge of honor. Being "the strong one" felt like purpose. Like identity. Like something to be proud of. People trusted me. People leaned on me. People expected me to come through. And I did. Every time.

But what nobody saw was how much it was costing me. Because while I was showing up for everyone else, I was slowly disappearing from myself.

There's a kind of exhaustion that sleep doesn't fix. It's not physical — it's deeper than that. It's the kind that settles in your spirit, the kind that makes you sit in silence longer than usual. Not because you want to, but because you don't have the energy to do anything else. That was me.

I remember one Saturday in particular. I had planned, prepared, led, and poured into every young person who walked through those doors. I smiled through every moment, answered every question, and made sure everything ran the way it was supposed to. And when it was finally over, I went to my car, changed my shoes, and just sat there for almost twenty minutes. Not because I was on the phone. Just sitting. Unable to make myself move. Because moving meant someone might need something else from me. And I had nothing left. That car became one of the most honest places I'd been in months.

There were nights I would sit on the edge of my bed, still dressed from the day, just staring. Not scrolling. Not watching TV. Not even thinking clearly. Just sitting. Trying to figure out when I started feeling like this. Trying to pinpoint the moment I went from living to just managing life.

When did joy become routine? When did passion become pressure? When did I start feeling like everything I did was something I had to do... instead of something I wanted to do?

From the outside, nothing looked wrong. I was functioning. I was producing. I was handling business. But internally, I felt stretched in every direction — pulled by responsibilities, drained by expectations, silenced by the need to keep it all together. And the hardest part? I didn't feel like I had permission to fall apart.

Because I had become "the strong one." And when you're the strong one, people don't check on you the same. They assume you're okay. They assume you've got it handled. They assume you don't need help. So you learn to carry things quietly. You learn how to smile through pressure. How to keep going when everything in you is asking for a pause.

I carried things I never talked about — the disappointments I brushed off, the prayers I whispered that seemed to go unanswered, the moments I felt overlooked, unsupported, or misunderstood. I carried the pressure of being consistent when I felt anything but steady. I pushed it down. Because that's what strong people do. At least, that's what I told myself.

But here's what I didn't realize at the time: just because you're functioning doesn't mean you're okay. Just because you're strong doesn't mean you're not struggling. And just because nobody sees it doesn't mean it's not heavy.

Even my prayers felt different. I still prayed — but it felt routine. Like I was going through the motions instead of having a real conversation with God. Busyness had become my defense. If I stayed in motion, I didn't have to sit with the parts of me that needed attention. God doesn't do His deepest work in the noise. He does it in the stillness. And I had been so afraid of what I might feel if I stopped that I kept running.

And performing looked different than people think. It was answering the text message with a smiley face when I was barely holding it together. It was saying "I'm good, just tired" when tired didn't even begin to cover it. Performance doesn't always look like a mask. Sometimes it looks like a really good Monday morning.

And if you're reading this and recognizing yourself — if something in these pages is hitting closer to home than you expected — I want you to know that I see you. Not the version of you that shows up and performs. I see the one underneath that. The one who is tired. The one who has been carrying things quietly. This book is for her.

You just know — something has to give. And whether you're ready or not, it will.

Reflect & Respond

1. When did you last feel truly empty — not just tired, but running on nothing? What were you doing when it hit you?

2. What does the 'strong one' role cost you that no one else sees? What have you been quietly carrying?

3. If a trusted friend asked you 'How are you really?' right now, what is the honest answer you've been holding back?

Chapter 2

Carrying What Was Never Mine

Somewhere along the way, I picked up things that were never mine to carry. It didn't happen all at once. There was no defining moment. It was subtle. A "yes" here when I should've said no. A moment of stepping in when I should've stepped back. A decision to help, fix, support, or hold things together — because I thought that's what I was supposed to do.

At first, it felt like strength. Like responsibility. Like maturity. And in many ways, it was. Because I cared. Because I showed up. But over time, what I picked up started picking me apart. I became the one people leaned on. The one they called when things went wrong. And I didn't mind that — at least, not at first. Because there's something about being needed that can make you feel valuable. Important. Seen. But what I didn't realize was that I wasn't just being helpful. I was becoming responsible for things that were never assigned to me. Other people's emotions. Other people's expectations. Other people's consequences. And I carried it all like it was mine.

I remember one night in particular. It was late — almost midnight — and I was on the phone talking someone through a situation that had nothing to do with me. My food was cold. I hadn't eaten since early that afternoon. I was tired in a way that went beyond that day. But I stayed on the phone. I listened. I gave what I had. And when I finally hung up, I sat in the quiet for a moment and realized — nobody had asked me how I was doing in weeks. And the painful part wasn't that they didn't ask. It was that I had made myself so available, so capable, so "on" — that it never even occurred to them that I might need someone to.

I carried conversations in my head that I never had out loud. I carried guilt for things I didn't cause. I carried pressure to fix situations I didn't break. That became my pattern. Check on everybody else. Show up for everybody else. Make sure everybody else is good. And then? Figure myself out later. But "later" never came.

I remember the exact feeling of almost saying no. The moment when something in me rose up and said, enough — and I opened my mouth, fully intending to set the boundary. And then I heard myself say, "I got it" instead. Not because anyone pressured me. But because the discomfort of disappointing someone felt bigger than the cost of abandoning myself. And that — that right there — was the pattern I hadn't named yet. I kept choosing everyone else's comfort over my own survival. And I called it being strong. But looking back now, I know what it really was. It was fear. Fear of being seen as selfish. Fear of being needed less. Fear of who I was if I wasn't the one holding everything together.

The more I carried for others, the less I had left for myself. I was present, but not fully there. Available, but emotionally drained. And my body already knew before my mind was willing to admit it. I was waking up tired even after a full night's sleep. My shoulders carried a tension I couldn't explain. Headaches I blamed on everything except the truth. My body was sending signals I didn't have time to listen to.

Beneath all the responsibility, beneath all the showing up, there was something building. Something I didn't want to look at too closely. Resentment. Not toward anyone specifically, but toward the weight itself. Toward the constant demand. And I had allowed that. That's the part I had to face. Because it wasn't just what people expected from me — it was what I expected from myself. I had created a standard I was now struggling to maintain.

And I think about that now — how many times God must have been watching me pick things up that He never placed in my hands. Whispering, "That one isn't yours." And I just couldn't hear Him. Not because He wasn't speaking — but because I had filled every quiet moment with doing, fixing, managing, and carrying. The weight I thought made me look strong was actually pulling me further from the place of rest He had been inviting me into all along.

You can't pour from an empty place forever. And I was getting closer to the moment where I would finally have to put it down.

Reflect & Respond

1. What are you currently carrying that was never really yours to pick up? How did you come to take it on?

2. Think of a moment you wanted to say no but said 'I got it' instead. What were you afraid would happen if you chose yourself?

3. What signals has your body been sending you that you've been ignoring? What would it mean to finally listen?

Chapter 3

The Performance Trap

I didn't realize I was performing. Not at first. Because when something becomes your normal, you don't question it. You just live it. And I had been living this way for so long that I didn't even recognize it for what it was.

I thought I was just being responsible. Just being dependable. Just showing up. But there's a difference between showing up and performing. And I was performing. Every day. It looked like smiling when I didn't feel like smiling. Saying "I'm good" when I wasn't. Keeping conversations light when my mind felt heavy. And the thing about performance is — it's exhausting. Not because you're doing something wrong, but because you're constantly managing how you show up. Managing your responses. Managing your emotions. Managing how much of yourself people get to see.

Performing wasn't something I invented as an adult. It was something I learned early. When you grow up understanding that certain emotions aren't welcome in certain spaces, you learn to manage them. When you figure out that being "too much" creates tension, you learn to shrink. When you discover that being needed feels safer than being seen, you learn to stay useful. I didn't decide to perform. I was trained to. And by the time I was old enough to question it, it already felt like survival.

I knew how to adjust. I could walk into a room and immediately read it. Feel the energy. Understand the expectations. Recognize what version of me needed to show up. I remember walking into a room one day, already exhausted before the conversation even started. Not because of what anyone had said—but because I already knew who I was about to be in that space. The listener. The helper. The one with the answers. And before anyone asked me anything...I had already adjusted.

That's when it hit me—this wasn't just who I was. It was who I had trained myself to be. And without even thinking about it, I would shift. Not intentionally, but automatically. Because somewhere along the way, I learned that who I was wasn't always what people needed. So I became who they did. And that worked. It helped me navigate. It helped me avoid conflict. But what it didn't do was allow me to be fully myself.

And what I didn't anticipate was how the performance affected the people around me too. The relationships I had were real — but they were built around the version of me I allowed people to see. And there's a loneliness in that. A specific kind of loneliness that's hard to name, because you're not alone. You're surrounded. You're loved. But you're not fully known. That fear kept me performing. Because being partially known felt safer than being fully seen and possibly rejected.

I remember one day specifically. Just a regular day. But I felt tired — not physically, but internally. And I paused and asked myself something I hadn't asked in a long time: why am I so tired? The answer, when it finally came, was simple. I was tired of showing up as someone I wasn't. Not completely, but enough that it was costing me. I was edited. Filtered. Adjusted. And that takes energy. More than you realize.

I also started noticing how this showed up in my faith. Because I wasn't just performing with people. I was performing with God. Even my prayers had become structured. Careful.

Polished. Like I was saying what I thought I was supposed to say, instead of what I actually felt. And it showed up in my ministry too. I could stand in front of young people and speak life into them — and mean every word of it. But there were moments when I walked away wondering if I was giving them something I hadn't fully received myself. It's a strange tension to live in — leading others toward a freedom you haven't fully stepped into yourself. And I don't say that with shame. I say it because I think more leaders live there than will ever admit it.

Because God already knew what I felt. What I was carrying. What I was avoiding. And yet I was still showing up like I had to present myself a certain way. And that created distance. Not because God moved, but because I wasn't being real. I used to wonder what it would feel like to just be. Not performing. Not managing. Not adjusting. Just present. Just real. Just me. And even imagining it felt foreign at first. But a part of me still believed that being fully known — by God, by myself, and eventually by others — was possible. And worth it.

And eventually, the performance would have to end.

Reflect & Respond

1. In what areas of your life do you perform rather than truly show up? What does your adjusted version look like compared to your real one?

2. Where did you first learn that certain parts of you weren't welcome? How has that shaped the way you move in rooms today?

3. What would it feel like to be fully known — not the edited version, but all of you? What are you most afraid people would see?

Chapter 4

Silent Battles No One Saw

There are some battles you don't talk about. Not because they don't matter, but because you don't know how to explain them. They don't have a clear beginning. They don't have a visible cause. They don't even always have words. They just exist. Quietly. Internally. That's where I was. Fighting battles no one could see. Not because I was trying to hide them, but because I didn't even fully understand them myself.

And that made the guilt worse. Because I kept thinking: what do I even have to complain about? I had people who loved me. I had purpose. I had a community. I had faith. From the outside, my life looked full. And I couldn't reconcile why something inside me felt so empty. So I dismissed it. Told myself it was ingratitude. But the emptiness didn't care about my blessings list. It stayed anyway.

I started noticing it in the quiet moments. Moments when there was nothing to do, no one to respond to, no expectation to meet. Those moments became uncomfortable. There were moments I would pick up my phone, scroll through messages, and realize I had responded to everyone...except myself. I knew how everyone else was doing. But if someone had asked me, in that exact moment, "How are you really?" I wouldn't have known how to answer. Because in the silence, everything I had been pushing aside started to surface. A heaviness I couldn't explain. A tension I couldn't shake. A sense that something wasn't right, even when everything looked fine.

I remember one evening sitting alone in a still room after the day was done. Everything had gone fine. I'd handled what needed to be handled. But I didn't feel accomplished. I felt drained. And not in a way that made sense. I sat there in the quiet, trying to understand why I didn't feel okay. And for the first time, I didn't rush past that feeling. I sat with it. And it was uncomfortable. Because I realized I had been avoiding myself. Avoiding what I felt. Avoiding what I needed. Because acknowledging it meant I couldn't keep moving the same way.

If I'm honest about what the battle actually sounded like — it was a lot of noise. Not loud, crashing noise. Just a constant low hum of thoughts that never fully quieted. Replaying conversations I should've handled differently. Wondering if I was doing enough. Worrying about things I had no control over. None of it was loud. All of it was exhausting. Because noise doesn't have to be deafening to wear you down. It just has to be constant.

That's what silent battles do. They don't announce themselves. They sit beneath the surface until you can't ignore them anymore. But I still kept it to myself. Because how do you explain something you don't fully understand? So I didn't say anything. I showed up like I always did. From the outside, nothing had changed. But inside, everything felt different.

And the loneliest part of a silent battle is that you fight it completely alone. Not because people aren't around. But because you've convinced yourself that no one would really understand. I had become so practiced at that divide — between what was happening inside and what I allowed people to see — that I almost forgot there was supposed to be a connection between the two.

I also noticed how it affected my relationship with God. I still prayed, but something felt off. Not wrong — just different. Like I was speaking but not fully connecting. I remember one night I just stopped pretending. I didn't have a beautiful prayer prepared. I just sat in the quiet and said honestly: "I don't know what's wrong with me. But something is. And I need You to meet me here." It wasn't elegant. But it was real. And I think that was the first genuinely honest moment I'd had with God in a long time. Something shifted in that stillness. Like He had been waiting for me to stop performing long enough to just be honest. And for the first time in a while, I didn't feel quite so alone in it.

Because silent battles don't stay silent forever. Eventually, they demand to be seen. And I was getting closer to that moment.

Reflect & Respond

1. What is the silent battle you've been fighting that no one knows about? What has kept you from naming it out loud?

2. Describe a moment when you said 'I'm fine' and meant the opposite. What did you really need in that moment?

3. What would it look like to stop performing in your prayers and be completely honest with God about where you are right now?

Chapter 5

When Exhaustion Became My Identity

At first, I thought I was just tired. The kind of tired that comes from doing a lot. From being busy. From handling responsibilities. From showing up day after day. It felt normal. Understandable. Even expected. Because life was full. And I was managing it.

But over time, that tiredness didn't go away. It didn't lift after a good night's sleep. It didn't reset after a weekend. It stayed. And not just physically. It settled deeper than that. It became emotional. Mental. Spiritual. It became something I carried with me everywhere. Rest stopped being restorative. I would sleep and wake up already tired. I would have a free day – genuinely free, nothing on the calendar – and spend most of it trying to recover from the week before, only to realize by evening that I still didn't feel rested. Because rest is supposed to replenish you. But mine wasn't working. And when rest stops working, it's usually because what you need isn't physical rest. It's something deeper. Something that sleep can't reach.

And at some point, I stopped saying "I'm tired" and started living like I am tired. That's the difference. Because there's a shift that happens when something you feel becomes something you believe. And I had crossed that line. I didn't just experience exhaustion anymore. I identified with it.

And the strange thing about losing yourself gradually is that you don't notice it happening in real time. It's not like a door slamming shut. It's more like a dimmer switch being turned down so slowly that by the time the room is dark, you've adjusted your eyes and convinced yourself the lighting is fine. I didn't wake up one day and not recognize myself. I just looked up one day and realized I had been running on dim for a long time. And somewhere along the way, dim had started to feel like enough.

I still showed up. That part didn't change. But I wasn't showing up the same way. There was a heaviness in everything I did. Even in moments that should've brought joy, I felt it. And I remember someone asking me once, genuinely, "Are you okay? You seem different." And for just a second, I almost told the truth. Almost let the wall come down. But instead I smiled and said, "I'm just a little tired, I'm fine." And the conversation moved on. And I stood there afterward thinking about how close I had come to being honest. And how quickly I had chosen not to be.

And that question had a spiritual weight to it too. So much of what I believed about myself was connected to what I did for God and for others. Being a leader. Being the one who showed up. That felt like purpose. So when I couldn't show up the same way, I started to wonder if I was failing not just myself, but God too. Those questions didn't have easy answers. But I've learned since that exhaustion is not a spiritual failure. It's a human signal. And God cares about both.

And even though I didn't know exactly what had to change or how it would happen, I could feel something shifting. That awareness was the beginning. Not of answers. But of honesty. And sometimes, honesty is the only first step you need.

Reflect & Respond

1. At what point did exhaustion stop being something you felt and start becoming something you identified with? What changed?

2. When someone asks how you're doing, what is the version you give — and what is the version that is actually true?

3. What would rest look like for you — real rest, not just recovery — if you gave yourself permission to have it?

Chapter 6

The Day Strength Ran Out

I didn't plan to break that day. There was nothing on my calendar that said: this is the day everything falls apart. It started like any other day. I woke up, got ready, moved through my routine. There was no warning. And maybe that's what made it hit harder. Because when you've been holding everything together for so long, you start to believe you always will.

But that morning had a different texture to it. I remember standing in the bathroom getting ready, looking at myself in the mirror, and not being able to muster the usual internal pep talk. The words felt hollow. Like I was saying them to someone I no longer fully believed in. And I should have taken that as a sign. But I didn't. I just put on my face — literally and figuratively — and kept moving.

There was a heaviness I couldn't shake. On the outside, everything looked the same. But inside, I felt like I was running on something I didn't have anymore. Like I was pulling from a place that was already empty. And then it happened. Not all at once. Not in some dramatic, obvious way. It was a small moment. Something that normally wouldn't have affected me the way it did. A conversation. A request. A situation that required me to show up again. And something in me just didn't respond the same way. I didn't have it. Not the energy. Not the patience. Not the strength I usually reached for without thinking.

So I tried to push through it. But this time, there was nothing to pull from. And that's when it hit me. Not just mentally, but physically. Emotionally. All at once. I felt it in my chest. Tight.

Heavy. My hands felt shaky. My breath was shorter than normal. And the most unsettling part was that I didn't feel sad about anything specific. I felt sad about everything at once. About all the years of holding it in. About all the times I chose everyone else first. About how long I had been living at a distance from my own heart. It all collapsed inward at the same time.

I stepped away. Not gracefully. Not with a plan. Just away. I found myself alone in my car — engine off, hands resting on the wheel, the day still visible through the windshield but feeling impossibly far away. I remember gripping the steering wheel tighter than I needed to. Like somehow holding on physically would keep everything else from falling apart. But it didn't. Because the truth was everything inside me had already started to.

And for the first time in a long time, I stopped. Completely. No distractions. No movement. No pretending. Because when it's quiet enough to hear yourself, you hear things you've been working hard not to hear. Things like: you're not okay. Things like: this is not sustainable. And in that silence, I couldn't argue with any of it. Because I knew it was all true.

And it came out. Not neatly. Just raw. Tears I didn't expect. Words I didn't plan. Emotions I had been avoiding for longer than I realized. Because for once, I didn't have the strength to hold it together. And that was new. Unfamiliar. Uncomfortable. But also real. Because I had spent so much time being strong that I didn't realize how much I needed to be honest.

And the truth was simple: I couldn't do it anymore. Not like this. Not carrying everything. Not pushing through everything. Not pretending everything was fine when it wasn't.

I sat there, tears falling, trying to understand how I got there. And the answer came quietly. I had been doing too much, for too long, without ever stopping. Without ever acknowledging that I needed help too. And it had caught up with me. All of it. The pressure. The expectations. The emotions I never processed. It had all built up until it had nowhere else to go. Except out.

And for me, the something deeper was God. Not the performative version of my faith. But the raw, unfiltered, nothing-left-to-prove version of me showing up before Him with empty hands. And saying: I don't have it. I never really had it. Not without You. That moment broke something open in me that I didn't know needed to be broken. Because I had been carrying things I was never meant to carry alone. And it took running completely out of strength to finally understand that His strength was never meant to be a supplement to mine. It was always meant to be the source.

And sometimes, that's where everything begins.

Reflect & Respond

1. Have you ever reached a moment where you had nothing left to give? What happened, and what did it reveal to you?

2. What emotions have you been holding in that might need to come out before real healing can begin?

3. What does 'empty hands before God' look like for you right now? What would you lay down if you believed He could hold it?

Part Two

The Breaking

Chapter 7

The Prayer That Wasn't Polished

After that moment, everything felt quiet. Not peaceful. Just still. Like something had finally stopped. I wasn't rushing anymore. Wasn't responding. Wasn't trying to gather myself together. I didn't have the energy to. And for the first time in a long time, I wasn't trying to fix how I felt. I just sat there. Letting it be what it was. Heavy. Real. Uncomfortable.

And naturally, my instinct was to pray. That's what I had always done. When things felt uncertain. When I needed clarity. When I needed strength. But this time it felt different. Because I didn't know what to say. And that scared me. Because I was used to having the words. Used to structuring my thoughts in a way that made sense. But now nothing felt structured. Nothing felt clear.

I had been performing my faith the same way I had been performing everything else. And the uncomfortable truth was that I hadn't even noticed. There's a difference between going through the motions of faith and actually bringing yourself to God. One is religious. The other is relational. And somewhere along the way, I had drifted from the relationship into the routine. I showed up. I said the words. But I hadn't been fully present with God in a long time. Because being fully present would have required me to be fully honest. And I wasn't ready for that. Until now.

And what came out wasn't polished. It wasn't structured. It wasn't even complete sentences at first. It was just real. "God..." I paused. Because even saying His name felt different. Like I wasn't coming to Him with answers. But with questions. With weight. With honesty I hadn't fully allowed myself to express before. "I'm tired." The words came out quietly. Almost like I wasn't sure if I should say them. But once I did, I couldn't stop. I'm tired of carrying everything. I'm tired of trying to hold it all together. I'm tired of feeling like I have to be strong all the time. And then the part I had been avoiding the most:

"I can't keep doing this like this."

That was the truth. Not dressed up. Not softened. Just real. Nothing shifted the way I expected. No voice. No sudden clarity. No overwhelming sense of direction. Just stillness. And I want to be honest about what that stillness felt like, because I think it matters. It didn't feel like peace — not at first. It felt like waiting in a room where you're not sure anyone is on the other side of the door. But then something settled in me. Not an answer. Just a reminder. That He hadn't moved. That the stillness wasn't absence. It was invitation.

And I realized something in that moment: this wasn't about getting an answer. This was about being honest. And that alone changed something. Not externally, but internally. Because for the first time, I wasn't trying to be strong in front of God. I wasn't trying to sound like I had it together. I was just me. Tired. Overwhelmed. Unsure. And somehow, that felt more right than anything I had said before. God already knew. He knew I was tired. He knew I was overwhelmed. And yet I had been showing up like I needed to pretend. And I didn't.

Surrender, I was learning, was the most active thing I had done in years. Because it required me to let go of control. And I had been holding on so tightly, for so long, that releasing it felt like losing something. It felt like stepping off solid ground. But the truth is, what I had been standing on wasn't solid ground. It was my own strength. And my own strength had already run out. Surrender wasn't the end of something. It was the beginning of standing on something that could actually hold me.

And if you've ever sat somewhere — on the edge of a bed, on the floor of a room — and felt like you didn't have the right words to pray, I want you to hear this: the unpolished prayer is still a prayer. The broken sentences still reach Him. The "I don't know what I need" is still an offering. God isn't waiting for you to get it together before you come to Him. He meets you in the middle of the falling apart. That's not a nice thought — it's the truth. And I needed to learn it for myself before I could say it to anyone else.

And sometimes, that's where everything starts.

Reflect & Respond

1. Have you ever felt like you didn't have the right words to pray? What was happening in that season?

2. What is the honest, unpolished prayer you've been afraid to pray? Write it here, exactly as it would come out.

3. Where in your faith have you been going through the motions instead of truly showing up? What would real presence look like?

Chapter 8

When God Feels Silent

I thought something would change after I prayed. Not everything. But something. A sense of direction. A feeling of clarity. A shift I could recognize. But when I got up, everything looked the same. The room hadn't changed. My situation hadn't changed. The weight I had been carrying was still there. And I didn't know what to do with that.

And I want to name something that I think a lot of people feel but rarely say out loud: I was disappointed. Not angry. Not faithless. Just disappointed. Because I had finally been real with God, I had let my guard down, I had stopped pretending. And the response I got was silence. Nobody prepares you for the moments when obedience doesn't feel like it comes with immediate reward. Nobody tells you that the breakthrough sometimes starts in a silence that feels a lot like being ignored. And sitting with that disappointment — without dismissing it, without performing through it — was one of the hardest things I had done yet.

I went through the rest of my day slower than usual. More aware. More intentional. Not because I had clarity, but because I didn't. And the more I tried to figure it out, the more frustrated I became. Because nothing was coming. No clear direction. No sudden understanding. Just silence. And silence can feel heavy when you're not used to sitting in it. Because silence doesn't give you anything to hold on to. It doesn't give you steps or answers or immediate reassurance. It just is.

I started doing something I hadn't done in a long time. I started writing. Not journaling in any structured way. Just words on a page. Things I was feeling that I didn't have anyone to say them to. Questions I was carrying that didn't have answers yet. And something about putting it on paper made it feel less like it was consuming me. I don't know if that was a spiritual practice or just survival. But it helped. And I think God meets us in our "just trying to get through it" moments just as much as He meets us in our polished ones.

And in that slowing down, I became more aware. Aware of how often I had tried to control things. How often I had tried to create clarity instead of waiting for it. I didn't trust silence. I trusted movement. I trusted action. I trusted doing something because it made me feel like I was in control. But silence required something different. It required trust. And that's where I struggled.

It was in that season that certain scriptures started landing differently than they ever had before. Not because I was studying harder. But because I was quieter. Psalm 46:10 — "Be still and know that I am God" — felt less like a command and more like an invitation. Like God saying: you don't have to figure this out. You just have to know who I am. And Matthew 11:28 — "Come to me, all you who are weary and burdened, and I will give you rest" — stopped being something I read and started being something I actually needed to receive. Because I finally understood what it felt like to be weary. Really, deeply weary. And to have nowhere else to bring it.

And I began to understand something: just because God is silent doesn't mean He is absent. That realization didn't come all at once. It came slowly. Through stillness. Through reflection. I wasn't being left alone. I was being taught something. Something I couldn't learn while everything was loud. Looking back now, I can see what that season was doing even when I couldn't see it in the moment. It was stripping away everything I had been using as a substitute for real trust. My productivity. My usefulness. My reputation as the one who handles things. All of it had become a way of feeling secure. And when all of that went quiet, I had to find out what was left. What I actually believed. Who I actually trusted.

And sometimes, that's where growth begins. Not in the answers. But in the waiting. In the silence. In the space where you don't have control, and you have to trust anyway.

Reflect & Respond

1. Have you ever felt like God was silent when you needed Him most? How did you respond to that silence?

2. What do you tend to reach for when God doesn't answer quickly — busyness, control, distraction? What is that telling you?

3. How would your relationship with God change if you trusted that His silence is not absence, but an invitation to go deeper?

Chapter 9

The Confrontation Within

Silence has a way of revealing things you've been avoiding. Not all at once. But slowly. Gently at first. And then clearly. That's what started happening to me. In the quiet moments — the ones I used to rush past — I started seeing things differently. Not around me. Within me.

Because it's one thing to recognize that life feels heavy. It's another thing to realize you've played a role in carrying that weight. That was the hard part. In the stillness, I started asking myself questions I hadn't asked before. Why do I keep saying yes when I'm already overwhelmed? Why do I feel responsible for things that aren't mine? Why do I keep pushing myself past my limits? Those questions didn't come with quick answers. They just sat there. And the more I thought about them, the more I realized something uncomfortable: this wasn't just about what was happening to me. This was about how I was responding to it. How I was allowing it. How I was participating in it.

And that realization didn't feel empowering at first. It felt heavy. Because it meant I couldn't just point outward anymore. I had to look inward. And looking inward requires honesty. The kind that says: this is where you've been contributing to your own exhaustion.

And I want to name something that doesn't get talked about enough in these kinds of moments: grief. Because when you realize that something you've been proud of — something that felt like a core part of who you are — has actually been hurting you, there's a grieving process that comes with that. I grieved the version of me that thought endurance was the same as strength. I grieved the years I spent running past my own needs. It wasn't anger. It was a quiet sadness. For the girl who learned to disappear into usefulness. And for how long I let her.

And when I got honest enough to trace them back, I realized most of those beliefs weren't things I chose. They were things I absorbed. From watching the women around me give until they had nothing left and call it love. From environments where being needed was praised and needing something was seen as weakness. I didn't develop these patterns in a vacuum. They were taught to me — sometimes directly, sometimes just by watching. And while I can't change where they came from, I had to decide whether I was going to keep living by beliefs that were never fully mine to begin with.

And for the first time, I wasn't trying to push past that realization. I was sitting in it. Fully. Honestly. And that's where the shift began. Not in my actions. Not yet. But in my awareness. Facing yourself is a practice. It's returning again and again to the questions that make you uncomfortable. It's being willing to sit in the tension of knowing something needs to change before you know exactly how to change it. Real self-confrontation is slower and messier than most of us are taught to believe.

And I want to say something about what that awareness felt like spiritually. Because it wasn't just psychological insight. It felt like light entering a room I had kept closed for a long time. And I believe that's what the Holy Spirit does when we finally get still enough to let Him work. He doesn't force the door open. He waits. And when you stop running long enough to sit in the quiet, He begins to show you things. Not to condemn you. But to free you. Because you cannot be healed from what you will not acknowledge. God was not showing me my patterns to shame me. He was showing me so I could finally be free from them.

Because sometimes the most powerful thing you can do is not fix everything. But finally face yourself. And I had done that. Not perfectly. Not completely. But honestly. And that honesty was the beginning of something new.

Reflect & Respond

1. What uncomfortable truth about yourself have you been avoiding? What would it mean to finally face it honestly?

2. Where did you first learn the patterns of over-giving or self-abandonment? What did you absorb from watching others?

3. What would it feel like to grieve the version of yourself who kept giving too much — not with shame, but with compassion?

Part Three

The Healing

Chapter 10

Letting It All Fall Apart

For a long time, I thought strength meant holding everything together. Keeping things in place. Keeping things moving. Keeping things from falling apart. That's what I had always done. No matter how I felt. No matter how heavy things became. I held it together. Because that's what I believed I was supposed to do.

But something had shifted. Not suddenly. Not suddenly. Not visibly. But deeply. Because after everything I had come to see, everything I had finally been honest about, I couldn't go back to pretending anymore. And that realization led me to a place I had never been before: I stopped trying to hold everything together.

At first, it didn't feel like strength. It felt like loss. Like I was letting things slip. Like I was failing in ways I had never allowed myself to before. Because when you've built your identity around being the one who keeps everything together, letting things fall feels wrong. Unnatural. Uncomfortable. But it was necessary. Because what I had been holding together was costing me too much.

I started small. Not with big decisions. Not with sweeping changes. But with moments. Moments where I paused instead of responding immediately. Moments where I didn't step in to fix something. Moments where I allowed something to be unresolved, even when everything in me wanted to handle it. My instinct was still there. The urge to step in. The urge to carry. It didn't disappear overnight. I had to choose differently. And choosing differently felt uncomfortable. It felt like I was going against who I had always been. But I wasn't. I was becoming someone new. And that process required letting go of who I used to be. Piece by piece.

I remember the first real no. Not a graceful one. Not a confident one. Just a quiet, uncomfortable, heart-racing no that I said before I could talk myself out of it. And the world didn't end. The person didn't fall apart. The situation worked itself out. And I stood there afterward feeling something I hadn't expected: relief. Not guilt. Relief. And that surprised me. Because I had spent so long believing that saying no would cost me something. But what I discovered was that saying yes to everything had already been costing me everything. The no just gave me back a small piece of myself. And I held onto it.

And people noticed. Not always in the ways I expected. Some people responded with genuine support. But others were thrown off. Because when you change the way you operate, the people who benefited from your old patterns sometimes don't know what to do with the new ones. A few pushed back. Some pulled away. And I had to make peace with that. Because not everyone will celebrate your boundaries. Some people will mourn the version of you that never had any. And that's painful. But it's also information. It tells you a lot about what the relationship was built on.

And as I let things fall, I realized something I hadn't expected: everything didn't collapse. The things I thought would fall apart didn't. The things I thought depended on me found their own way. And that was eye-opening. Because it showed me something I hadn't fully believed before: I didn't have to carry everything for things to function.

And spiritually, letting go looked like releasing the need to have everything figured out before I moved forward. It looked like trusting God with outcomes I couldn't control. It looked like praying differently — not just asking Him to fix things, but asking Him to show me what I needed to release. There's a version of faith that grips tightly to a plan and calls it trust. And then there's the version that opens its hands and says: whatever this becomes, I believe You're in it. I was learning the second kind. Because real trust doesn't need a guaranteed outcome. It just needs to believe that God is present in the process.

And I want to say this clearly, because I think it matters: making room is an act of faith. It can look like stepping back. Like doing less. Like being quieter than you used to be. But what it actually is — what it was for me — was preparation. You cannot receive what your hands are too full to hold. You cannot become who God is calling you to be while still fully inhabiting who you used to be. Something has to shift. Something has to be released. And sometimes that release looks like falling apart from the outside. But from the inside? It's the beginning of being rebuilt.

What feels like falling apart is sometimes everything falling into place. And I was finally learning to let it.

Reflect & Respond

1. What is one thing you've been holding together that you may need to let fall? What are you afraid will happen if you let go?

2. Describe your first real no. How did it feel before you said it, and what happened after?

3. What has been the cost of always saying yes? What has it taken from you that you'd like to reclaim?

Chapter 11

Healing in Hidden Places

After I stopped trying to hold everything together, there was space. At first, it felt unfamiliar. Quiet in a way I wasn't used to. Not empty. Just open. And in that openness, something began to surface. Not pressure. Not expectations. But what had been underneath all along. Me.

Not the version of me that knew how to show up for everyone else. Not the version of me that carried everything. But the version of me that had been pushed aside. That part of me didn't come rushing back. It revealed itself slowly. In quiet moments. In pauses. In the absence of everything that used to fill my time and energy.

And reconnecting with yourself is a stranger process than you might expect. Because you'd think you'd know yourself. But when you've spent years adjusting yourself to fit what everyone else needs, you start to lose the thread. You forget what you actually enjoy versus what you've just learned to tolerate. You forget what brings you real joy versus what just feels productive. And rediscovering those things — slowly, without pressure — was one of the most unexpectedly healing parts of this season.

And I realized something: healing isn't loud. It doesn't announce itself. It doesn't come with immediate results. It happens in quiet places. In moments no one else sees. In decisions no one else notices. In shifts that aren't obvious from the outside, but are deeply felt within. That's where I was. In a hidden place. Not isolated. But intentional. Because for the first time, I wasn't trying to fill every moment. I wasn't rushing to the next thing. I was sitting with it.

And that required something I hadn't practiced before: patience. Not with others. With myself. Because healing doesn't happen on a timeline you can control. It doesn't follow a schedule. There were days I felt lighter. More present. More connected. And then there were days where the heaviness returned. Not as strong as before, but enough to remind me I was still in the process. And on those days, I had to learn something important: a hard day is not evidence that you haven't healed. It's evidence that you're still human. And that's okay.

Rest isn't a reward. It's a requirement. And I had been neglecting it for too long. So I honored it. Even when it felt uncomfortable. Even when my mind told me I should be doing something else. I chose stillness. And in that stillness, I began to reconnect with myself. Not in an obvious way. But in small, meaningful ways. Moments where I felt present again. Moments where I felt clarity. Moments where I didn't feel like I was just moving through life, but actually experiencing it.

And as I found my way back, I started noticing things returning. Small things. A genuine laugh — not the performed kind, but the kind that surprised me. Curiosity about things that had nothing to do with being productive or helpful. The ability to sit in a moment and actually be in it. I started enjoying things again. And that noticing mattered more than I can explain. Because it told me something I had started to forget: I was still in there. Underneath all the exhaustion and the performance and the weight. She was still there. And she was coming back.

I also noticed something in my relationship with God. It felt different. Not distant anymore. But quieter. Less about asking. More about being. I didn't feel the need to say as much. I didn't feel the need to explain everything. I just sat. And that was enough. Because God was with me in the quiet too. Not just in the moments of breakthrough. But in the waiting. In the stillness. In the process.

And what healing in hidden places taught me is that the most important work often doesn't have an audience. One day, I chose to sit down instead of immediately responding to a message. That might not sound like much. But for me, it was everything. Because for the first time, I didn't abandon myself to show up for someone else.

Nobody was clapping for the moment I chose to rest instead of respond to one more request. Nobody saw the morning I woke up and didn't immediately reach for my phone. Nobody witnessed the quiet decision to stay home when every part of me would've previously pushed through. But God saw it. And I felt it. And that was enough. Because not everything meaningful needs to be witnessed to be real. Some of the most significant growth happens in moments that will never make it into a highlight reel. And those moments — the small, private, intentional ones — were building something in me that the loud seasons never could.

Because sometimes progress isn't loud. It's not loud or obvious. It doesn't announce itself. Sometimes it's just the quiet realization that you're finally healing.

Reflect & Respond

1. What does your hidden healing look like — the work no one sees, the small choices only you and God know about?

2. What is something you've rediscovered about yourself in a quiet season that you had forgotten or pushed aside?

3. What would it mean for you to choose yourself in one small, private way today? What would that look like?

Chapter 12

Learning to Breathe Again

It didn't happen all at once. There wasn't a moment where everything suddenly felt different. No clear line where I could say: this is where it changed. It was quieter than that. Subtle. But noticeable. Like something inside me was beginning to shift in a way I hadn't felt in a long time.

At first, I didn't trust it. Because I had been in a heavy place for so long that lightness felt unfamiliar. Almost foreign. Like something I wasn't sure how to hold onto. When you've lived in heaviness for a long time, lightness doesn't always feel like relief at first. It can feel like a trap. I had been so accustomed to bracing for the next hard thing that I didn't know how to simply receive a moment of ease. But slowly, as the lightness kept returning, I started to let myself believe it was real. Not permanent in a naïve way. But present. And that was enough.

I noticed it one morning. I woke up and for a few seconds, I didn't feel the weight. There was no immediate rush of thoughts. No list of responsibilities pressing in. No sense of heaviness sitting on my chest. Just stillness. And for a moment, I just laid there. Not because I was exhausted. But because I was aware. Aware that something felt lighter. And I didn't want to rush past it.

And I started noticing it in other places too. In my thoughts. They weren't as overwhelming. I wasn't overthinking every little thing. I wasn't replaying conversations in my head. There was space. Space between thoughts. Space to breathe. And that space changed how I moved. Because I wasn't reacting the same way anymore. I wasn't rushing. I wasn't forcing things. I was allowing things to be. And in that allowing, I found something I didn't realize I had lost. Peace. Not the kind of peace that comes from everything being perfect. But the kind that comes from being aligned. From not fighting yourself. From not carrying more than you're supposed to.

I also noticed something else. I was starting to enjoy things again. Not in a forced way. But naturally. There were moments where I laughed and it didn't feel like I was trying. Moments where I smiled and it came from a real place. And something else started happening that I hadn't expected: a real, quiet, almost surprised gratitude. For ordinary things. For a morning that felt still. For a laugh that caught me off guard. For a meal I actually tasted instead of just consuming between responsibilities. These were small things. But they were mine. And noticing them felt like being given something back.

I also noticed how it showed up in my body. I wasn't as tense. My shoulders didn't feel as tight. My breathing felt different. Deeper. Slower. More natural. Like my body was finally catching up to what my mind and spirit were beginning to experience. And practically, learning to breathe again looked like small, deliberate acts of permission. Permission to leave something undone. Permission to say "I don't have the capacity for that today" without a lengthy explanation. These weren't grand gestures. They were quiet choices. But each one was a breath.

I also felt a shift in my relationship with God. It wasn't about asking for things anymore. It wasn't about needing answers right away. It was about connection. Simple. Steady. Real. I found myself sitting in quiet moments not because I was searching for something, but because I wanted to be there. Before, quiet felt uncomfortable. Now it felt safe. Like a place I could rest.

And when survival mode ends, you discover things about yourself that the pressure had been covering up. I discovered that I actually had opinions about things that had nothing to do with being helpful. I discovered that I enjoyed quiet mornings in a way that wasn't about recovering from something, but just about being in them. I discovered that I was creative again — not in the structured, output-driven way I had been performing creativity, but in a freer, more exploratory way. And I discovered that I was funny. Not in the managed, make-everyone-comfortable way, but genuinely, spontaneously funny. And laughing at my own thoughts felt like reclaiming something I hadn't even realized I'd given away. These weren't small discoveries. They were evidence of a woman coming back to herself. And I welcomed every single one.

And I was finally learning what that felt like. One breath at a time.

Reflect & Respond

1. When did you last feel genuinely light — not performing lightness, but actually experiencing it? What made it possible?

2. What small moments of joy or presence have you been rushing past? What would it look like to stay in them?

3. What is one thing you've discovered about yourself now that the noise has quieted — something that surprised you?

Chapter 13

Boundaries Without Guilt

At first, setting boundaries felt wrong. Not just uncomfortable. Wrong. Like I was doing something I wasn't supposed to do. Like I was stepping outside of who I had always been. Because for so long, I had been the one who said yes. Yes to helping. Yes to showing up. Yes to being available. Even when it cost me. Even when I didn't have the capacity. Even when I knew, deep down, I needed to pause.

And for a long time, I met those expectations. Without question. Without pause. Without considering what it was doing to me. But something had shifted. And that meant I had to start making different choices. Moments where I paused. Moments where I asked myself: do I actually have the capacity for this? And sometimes the answer was no. And saying no felt heavy. Not because it was wrong, but because it was new. Because I wasn't just saying no to a request. I was saying no to a version of myself that had always said yes.

That wasn't easy. Because every time I said no, guilt showed up immediately. Questions followed: what if they're disappointed? What if they think I've changed? What if they need me? But I had to learn something: guilt doesn't always mean you're doing something wrong. Sometimes it means you're doing something different. And different feels uncomfortable before it feels right.

So I sat with that. The discomfort. The questions. The urge to go back to what felt familiar. And instead of giving in, I stayed with the decision. And something started to happen. The guilt didn't disappear immediately. But it softened. Because I realized something: the world didn't fall apart when I said no. Things still moved. People still found solutions. Situations still resolved without me carrying them.

And that realization shifted something in me. Because I had believed that I was needed in a way that required me to always show up. But that wasn't true. I was valued, but I wasn't responsible for everything. And once I understood that, it became easier to set boundaries. Not perfectly. But intentionally. I also started to communicate differently. Not with long explanations. Not with over-justification. But with clarity. Simple. Direct. Because not every decision requires an explanation. Sometimes clarity is enough.

And the more I practiced that, the more confident I became. Not loud confidence. Not defensive confidence. But quiet certainty. The kind that doesn't need approval. The kind that simply knows: this is what I need. And I started protecting that. Not aggressively. But intentionally. In my time. In my energy. In my availability.

And I realized something: boundaries don't push people away. They position you correctly. They show people how to engage with you. They define what is acceptable and what isn't. And most importantly, they protect your peace. Something I had never prioritized before. But now it was non-negotiable. Because I understood what it felt like to not have it. And I wasn't going back to that.

A wall and a boundary are not the same thing. A wall keeps everyone out. It's built from pain, and its goal is protection through distance. A boundary is something different. It's not about keeping people away. It's about defining how you can be in relationship with them in a way that doesn't cost you yourself. Walls say: I don't trust you. Boundaries say: I value this relationship enough to be honest about what I can and cannot give. And when I started setting boundaries from that place — not from fear or resentment, but from clarity and care — I wasn't closing people out. I was finally showing up with something real to offer.

Because I understood something now: if I don't protect my peace, no one else will. And I was finally willing to take responsibility for that.

Reflect & Respond

1. What boundary do you need to set but haven't yet? What is keeping you from setting it?

2. What is the difference between a wall and a boundary in your own life? Where have you confused the two?

3. After holding a boundary recently, did you feel guilt or peace? What was that telling you?

Chapter 14

Reintroducing Myself to Myself

After everything slowed down, after I stopped carrying what wasn't mine, after I started setting boundaries, after I created space for myself, there was something I didn't expect: I didn't fully recognize myself anymore. Not in a negative way. But in a way that made me pause. Because for so long, I had defined myself by what I did. By how I showed up. By what I handled. By how much I could carry. That was my identity. And now I wasn't operating from that place anymore.

And the question of who am I without all of that didn't come with an immediate answer. Because I had spent so much time being who I needed to be for everyone else that I hadn't taken the time to discover who I was for myself. And now that I had the space to do that, it felt unfamiliar. Almost like meeting someone new. Someone I should know, but didn't fully understand yet.

So I started paying attention. Not to what I needed to do, but to what I naturally felt drawn to. What felt good. What felt aligned. What didn't require effort to maintain. And those things were different than what I was used to. I noticed that I enjoyed quiet more. Not because I was tired, but because I was at peace. I didn't feel the need to fill every moment with something. I didn't feel uncomfortable in stillness anymore.

And I want to name how strange that stillness felt at first. Because I had spent years filling space. Every quiet moment was an opportunity to respond to something, fix something, plan something. Stillness had always felt like a gap to be closed. But now it was becoming something else. It was becoming the place where I could actually hear myself. Where my own thoughts had room to exist without being crowded out by everyone else's needs. And learning to listen again — to my own instincts, my own preferences, my own needs — felt like turning up the volume on something that had been muted for a very long time.

And one of the most unexpected parts of that reconnection was rediscovering what I actually liked. Not what was useful. Not what made me more helpful. But what I genuinely enjoyed for no other reason than that it brought me something. Some of those things were things I hadn't done in years. Some were things I had dismissed as unnecessary. But they weren't unnecessary. They were mine. And reclaiming them felt like reclaiming pieces of a self I had quietly surrendered over years of focusing outward.

I also noticed something in how I saw myself. I wasn't measuring my worth the same way. I wasn't asking: did I do enough? Did I show up enough? Did I meet expectations? Those questions didn't hold the same weight anymore. Instead I was asking: did this feel right? Was I aligned? Did I honor myself? And those questions changed everything. Because they shifted my focus from external validation to internal alignment. And that's where identity is truly formed. Not in what you do for others, but in how you show up for yourself.

And in that season, I started going back to what God says about who I am. Not what I do. Not what I carry. But who I am. That I am fearfully and wonderfully made. That I am known before I was formed. That I am chosen, loved, and seen — not because of my output, but because of my belonging. And I had to sit with those truths in a new way. Because I had always read them and moved on quickly, back to doing and managing and showing up. But now I had to actually receive them. To let them land. To let them mean something about how I treated myself.

And if you're in a season where you don't fully recognize yourself, I want to say something to you directly: that's not a crisis. It might actually be the beginning of something. Because sometimes you have to lose the version of yourself that was built for everyone else before you can find the one that was made for you. The woman emerging on the other side of your exhaustion, your surrender, your letting go — she's not a stranger. She's the most honest version of you. And she's worth getting to know. Take your time. Pay attention. Ask yourself the questions you've been skipping. Because it's you. The real one. And she's been there all along.

And that's where I was. Reintroducing myself to myself. And this time, I was paying attention.

1. Who are you when no one needs anything from you? What comes naturally, what brings you joy, what do you actually want?

2. What parts of yourself did you quietly surrender over the years while focusing on everyone else? How do you begin to reclaim them?

3. What does God say about who you are — not what you do, but who you are — and how well have you actually received it?

Chapter 15

Faith That Feels Different Now

My faith didn't disappear during everything I went through. But it did change. Not suddenly. Not in a way I could clearly define at first. But over time, I began to notice it. In how I prayed. In how I thought. In how I responded to things I didn't understand. It felt different. Not weaker. But quieter. Less emotional. Less reactive.

And I want to pause here and name something I think a lot of people experience and never talk about: the quiet faith crisis. Not the dramatic kind where you walk away from everything. But the slow, disorienting kind where things still look the same on the outside — you still show up, you still serve, you still say the right things — but something on the inside has shifted and you don't know what to call it. I was in that. And the reason nobody talks about it is because it doesn't look like a crisis. It looks like a Sunday morning. It looks like leading youth. It looks like prayer. But underneath, you're quietly asking: is this real for me anymore? And the honest answer I had to sit with was: I don't know. And sitting in that not knowing, without performing around it, was one of the most important things I had ever done.

Because before, I trusted God when I felt Him. When things made sense. When I could see movement. But now I trusted Him even when I didn't feel anything. Even when things were unclear. Even when I didn't have answers. And that's a different kind of faith. Not one that depends on emotion. But one that stands on truth. Because feelings change. They come and go.

But truth remains. And I had learned to anchor myself in that. Not because it was easy. But because it was necessary.

And mature faith, I was learning, looks less like certainty and more like steadiness. It doesn't mean you have everything figured out. It doesn't mean you never doubt. It means that when the doubt comes, you don't run from it. You bring it to God instead of away from Him. It means you can say "I don't understand this" and still trust the character of the One you're talking to. It means you can be honest about what you're feeling without letting your feelings become the final authority on what's true.

I also found myself praying differently. Not longer. Not more structured. But more honest. More present. More real. I didn't feel the need to say everything perfectly. I didn't feel the need to sound a certain way. I just spoke from where I was. And that honesty deepened my relationship with God. Because I wasn't holding anything back. I wasn't filtering my thoughts. I was just real. And that's where connection happens. Not in perfection. But in truth.

And in this season, there were a few scriptures that became anchors for me in a way they hadn't been before. Not because I was studying harder. But because I was quieter. Isaiah 40:31 – "But those who hope in the Lord will renew their strength" – stopped being a motivational phrase and started feeling like a promise I actually needed. Because I had tried to renew my own strength for years. And it hadn't worked. And Proverbs 3:5–6 – "Trust in the Lord with all your heart and lean not on your own understanding" – had new weight when I read it in that season. Because I had spent years leaning on my own understanding. And it had run out. What I was learning was that the instruction to trust wasn't a passive one. It was an active, daily, sometimes difficult choice.

And I began to understand something: just because God is silent doesn't mean He is absent. This version of faith wasn't dependent on how I felt. It wasn't shaken by what I didn't understand. It wasn't weakened by waiting. It was rooted. And that root held me. Through uncertainty. Through silence. Through everything I had walked through. And I want to say what that kind of faith produces. Because it's not just peace. It's perspective. You start to see difficulty as something that can be moved through rather than something you'll be buried under. You start to see waiting as formation rather than abandonment. You start to see silence as presence rather than absence. And sometimes, that's the only change that matters.

And that's the kind of faith that doesn't break.

Reflect & Respond

1. How has your faith changed through what you've walked through? Is it stronger, quieter, more honest — or something else?

2. Have you ever experienced a quiet faith crisis — still showing up on the outside while questioning on the inside? What was that like?

3. What scripture has landed differently for you in a hard season? What did it mean to you then, and what does it mean now?

Part Four

The Becoming

Chapter 16

The Separation Season

I didn't decide to distance myself from everything all at once. It wasn't a single defining moment. No big announcement. No clear line where I said: this no longer belongs in my life. It happened gradually. Quietly. In ways that didn't feel forced, but felt necessary. Because as I began to change, as I began to think differently, as I began to move differently, I started to notice something: everything around me didn't feel the same anymore. Not wrong. Just different.

At first, I questioned it. Because I didn't want to assume something was wrong. I didn't want to create distance where it didn't need to be. So I stayed present. I observed. I paid attention. And the more I did, the clearer it became. This wasn't about something being wrong. This was about something no longer fitting. And that's a different kind of realization. Because when something doesn't fit anymore, you can't force it to.

And I want to be honest about what that hardness felt like. Because outgrowing a relationship — even when it's no one's fault — carries its own kind of grief. It's not the same as a falling out. It's quieter than that. It's realizing that someone who was once central to your story is now more on the periphery. It's caring about someone and still feeling the distance. And that grief doesn't always get acknowledged because there's no clear moment of loss. But it's real. And I had to give myself permission to feel it, without using it as a reason to go backward.

And that's what this season was about. Release. Not rejection. Not isolation. But alignment. And I want to be clear about what this season was not. It wasn't bitterness. It wasn't me deciding that people or things from my past were bad. It wasn't me building walls or closing myself off. It was simply the natural result of becoming more honest about what I needed. And when you become more honest about what you need, some things stop fitting. Not because they were wrong. But because you've grown into something different. And growth, by definition, means you can't stay the same size.

And spiritually, I started to understand this season differently too. Because in scripture, separation seasons are not uncommon. There are moments all throughout the Bible where God calls someone away from the familiar and into something new. Abraham leaving his homeland. Ruth leaving Moab. David in the wilderness before the palace. These weren't punishments. They were preparations. And I began to see my own separation season through that lens. Not as something happening to me. But as something being done for me. God was creating the conditions for something I couldn't build in the middle of everything I used to be surrounded by. The space wasn't empty. It was intentional.

And what I found in that space surprised me. I expected loneliness. And there were moments of that. But mostly, I found clarity. Without the constant noise of conversations and commitments and connections that no longer fit, I could hear myself more clearly. I could hear God more clearly. I started to see what I actually wanted — not what I had settled for, not what I had maintained out of loyalty, but what I actually wanted for my life going forward. And that vision, however incomplete, gave me something to move toward. Not just away from what no longer fit. But toward what was becoming.

Because I understood something now: growth requires separation. Not always from people. But from patterns. From habits. From mindsets. From versions of yourself that no longer align with who you're becoming. And I was in that process. Not rushing it. Not forcing it. Just allowing it. And trusting that where I was being led was better than where I had been. Even if I couldn't fully see it yet.

And sometimes, that trust is enough to keep moving forward.

Reflect & Respond

1. Is there a relationship, habit, or environment in your life that no longer fits who you are becoming? How do you know?

2. What grief have you felt — quietly, without a clear reason — as you've grown beyond certain seasons or people?

3. How are you learning to trust that what God is separating you from is not punishment, but preparation?

Chapter 17

Standing in Who I've Become

There was a time when I questioned everything about myself. Not out loud. Not in a way anyone else could see. But internally, I was unsure. Unsure of what I felt. Unsure of what I needed. Unsure of how I should move. I second-guessed my decisions. Because for so long, I had been defined by how I responded to everything around me. By how I adjusted. By how I carried. By how I made things work. And when that started to change, so did my confidence.

Not because I had lost it, but because I was learning how to rebuild it differently. Not based on what I could handle, but based on who I actually was. And rebuilding confidence from the inside out looks different than I expected. I thought it would feel like a return. But it wasn't a return. It was a construction. Something entirely new being built from materials I had never used before. Things like self-trust. And self-knowledge. And the willingness to sit with uncertainty without immediately reaching for reassurance. That kind of work doesn't happen quickly. But it happens. And when it does, what you build is something that doesn't crumble when circumstances change.

But now something felt different. Not suddenly. But clearly. I wasn't questioning myself the same way anymore. I wasn't overthinking every decision. I wasn't looking outside of myself for confirmation. I was moving with a quiet certainty. And that certainty wasn't loud. It didn't need to be. Because it wasn't about proving anything. It was about knowing. Knowing what felt right. Knowing what didn't. Knowing when to say yes and when to say no. Without over-explaining. Without second-guessing. Without guilt.

I wasn't carrying expectations the same way. Not from others. And not from myself. I was standing in who I had become. And that required something: ownership. Ownership of my growth. Ownership of my choices. Ownership of the person I was now. Without apology. Without hesitation. Because growth isn't about being understood. It's about being aligned. And I was aligned. With my decisions. With my boundaries. With my faith. With myself. And that alignment gave me a sense of peace I couldn't fake. A steadiness that didn't require validation. A confidence that didn't need to be announced.

And that's a different kind of strength. Not the kind that pushes through everything. But the kind that stands firm. Grounded. Unshaken. Certain. The old strength was impressive from the outside. It could carry enormous weight. But it was also exhausting. And brittle in ways that weren't visible until something finally cracked it. This new strength looks quieter. It doesn't announce itself. It doesn't need to carry everything to prove it exists. But it is far more durable. Because it's not built on capacity. It's built on character. On the slow, unsexy work of knowing yourself, honoring yourself, and trusting something larger than yourself. And that kind of strength doesn't run out the way the old kind did. It sustains.

And I want to say something about what it means to stand. Because standing isn't passive. Standing is a choice you make in the face of everything that's trying to pull you back. Standing means that when the old guilt shows up, you don't give it the same seat at the table. When someone expects the old version of you and pushes back against the new one, you don't collapse.

Standing isn't about being unmovable. It's about being rooted. Rooted enough that when the wind comes — and it will come — you bend without breaking. And you come back to yourself. Every time.

And sometimes I think about the woman I was at the beginning of all this. The one sitting on the edge of the bed, still dressed from the day, too exhausted to move. The one showing up for everyone while quietly disappearing from herself. The one who didn't know how to ask for help because she had trained everyone, including herself, to believe she didn't need it. And I want to say something to her. I would tell her: it's coming. The clarity is coming. The rest is coming. The version of you that doesn't need to perform to feel valuable — she's already in you. She's just waiting for you to stop long enough to meet her. And when you do, you won't recognize how you lived without her. Hold on. It's coming.

And for the first time in a long time, I felt like myself. Not the version shaped by pressure. Not the version shaped by expectations. But the version shaped by growth. By truth. By alignment. And that version? She wasn't going anywhere.

Reflect & Respond

1. How do you define confidence now compared to how you defined it before your breaking point? What is the difference?

2. In what areas of your life are you still seeking outside approval for decisions you already know are right?

3. What would it look like to stand firmly in who you've become — even when others still expect the old version of you?

Chapter 18

The Life I Don't Have to Escape From

There was a time when I needed an escape. Not always physically. But mentally. Emotionally. Spiritually. I needed moments where I could step away from everything just to feel like I could breathe. Because my life, as it was, felt heavy. Not because everything was falling apart. But because I was carrying too much of it. And I want to be honest about what that escape actually looked like for me. Because It wasn't anything obvious. It was staying so busy that I didn't have to feel anything. It was scrolling mindlessly because stillness felt dangerous. It was saying yes to one more commitment because being needed felt safer than being empty. It was staying in motion because the moment I stopped, everything I had been avoiding would catch up to me. That's what my escape looked like. And for a long time, I didn't even recognize it as escape. I called it productivity. I called it responsibility. But it was avoidance dressed in a very convincing costume.

But the problem with escape is that it's temporary. You leave for a moment, but everything is still there when you come back. And for a long time, that's how I lived. Managing. Handling. Escaping when I could. Returning when I had to. Repeating the cycle. But now something had changed. Not everything around me. But everything within me. Because I wasn't carrying things the same way anymore. And because of that, my life felt different. Not lighter because there was nothing to do. But lighter because I wasn't doing everything.

I noticed I wasn't rushing anymore. Not to respond. Not to fix. Not to prove anything. And the quiet felt different this time. It didn't feel heavy. It felt like peace.

There was space. Space in my mind. Space in my time. Space in my energy. And that space changed how I experienced my life. I didn't feel the need to escape anymore. I was living in a way that felt sustainable. And that's different. Because sustainability means you don't need to run from your life. You can stay in it. Fully. Presently. Without feeling like you need a break from it every moment. And I had never experienced that before.

And I want to describe what presence actually feels like, because I think it's different than people expect. It's not a dramatic awakening. It's not a constant state of mindful bliss. It's smaller than that. It's finishing a conversation and realizing you were actually in it. It's eating a meal and tasting the food. It's driving somewhere and noticing the sky. It's laughing and not immediately cataloguing everything you still have to do. Those are the moments I started noticing. Small. Unspectacular. But completely different from the way I had been moving through my life. And I held onto each one, because they were evidence of something I had been working toward without fully knowing it: a life I didn't need to mentally leave.

I also noticed how my relationship with rest had changed. Before, rest felt like something I had to earn. Something I only allowed myself after everything else was done. But now rest was part of my life. Not separate from it. Not something I had to justify. Just something I allowed. Because I understood its value. And I honored it. Without guilt. Without overthinking. And that made a difference. Because I wasn't constantly running on empty anymore. I was replenishing as I moved. And that created sustainability. The kind I had never experienced before.

I also realized something deeper: peace isn't something you visit. It's something you build. Through your decisions. Through your boundaries. Through what you choose to carry and what you don't. And I had built that. Not overnight. But through everything I had learned. Through everything I had released. And now I was living in it. Staying in peace requires continued intention. It's more like a garden. You have to tend to it. You have to keep choosing the things that built it in the first place. The boundaries. The honesty. The rest. The willingness to say no when you need to. The commitment to not pick up what you've already put down. Peace isn't a destination you reach and then stop working. It's a way of living you keep choosing. Every day.

And I want to say something about what comes next. Because this isn't the end of a story. It's a foundation for a new one. Everything I've walked through — the exhaustion, the breaking, the silence, the surrender, the slow and often unseen rebuilding — all of it has prepared me for something. I'm not approaching what's next from empty hands anymore. I'm approaching it from a place of wholeness. From clarity. From a settled sense of who I am and what I'm actually called to carry. The best chapters of your story often come after the hardest ones. Not in spite of the hard ones. But because of them. And I believe that. For myself. And for you.

And for the first time, I wasn't trying to escape my life. I was living it. Fully. Presently. Peacefully.

Reflect & Respond

1. What did your escape look like — busyness, scrolling, over-committing, staying in motion? How long did it work?

2. What does it feel like to live in a way that doesn't require escape? Are you there yet, or still moving toward it?

3. What daily choices build the peace you want to live in? What practices or boundaries protect it?

Chapter 19

This Version of Me Was Worth Becoming

When I look back now, I see it differently. Not the details. Not the moments themselves. But the meaning behind them. Because when I was in it, I didn't understand. I didn't understand why everything felt so heavy. Why I was carrying so much. At the time, it just felt like life. Something to get through. Something to manage. Something to survive. And I did. I survived it. But survival wasn't the point. That's what I see now.

Because everything I went through — every moment of exhaustion, every moment of confusion, every moment where I felt like I was reaching my limit — it was all shaping something. Not around me. Within me. And I couldn't see that then. But now I can see it. Clearly. Because I'm no longer in it. I'm beyond it. And perspective changes everything.

And I want to be specific about what looks different from this side. Because when you're in the middle of a hard season, you can't see the shape of it. You only see what's directly in front of you. But from the other side, you see the whole arc. You see that the season had a purpose. You see that the things that felt like interruptions were actually redirections. You see that the moments that stripped you down were the moments that prepared you. And you see that the version of you who came through it — quieter, slower, more honest, more grounded — is more capable than the one who was performing strength before the breaking point. That version could do a lot. But she was running on fumes. This one is running on something real.

I can also see how I lost myself. Not intentionally. Not suddenly. But gradually. Through every time I ignored what I felt. Through every time I pushed past my limits. Through every time I chose to show up for everyone else without showing up for myself. And that realization could've been hard to sit with. But I didn't stay there. Because I also see something else: I found myself again. Not the same version. But a better one. A more aligned one. A version of me that understands herself. That honors herself. That moves differently. And that version? She was worth becoming.

And I want to say something about comparison. Because one of the things that made this journey harder was measuring where I was against where I used to be. Wondering why I couldn't show up the way I used to. And the answer — which I understand now but didn't then — is that the old capacity was built on patterns that were unsustainable. I wasn't becoming less capable. I was refusing to keep exceeding my actual limits. And those are very different things. Growth sometimes looks like doing less. Because you're finally doing the right things.

And there's a specific kind of gratitude that comes with that. Not the kind that pretends the hard parts weren't hard. But the kind that says: I needed this. Not the pain for its own sake. But what the pain produced. The clarity I wouldn't have found without the crisis. The faith I wouldn't have developed without the silence. The boundaries I wouldn't have set without the breakdown. The version of myself I wouldn't have become without all of it. I'm grateful for the process in the way you're grateful for a surgery that saved your life — not because you enjoyed it, but because you understand now what it made possible. And I wouldn't trade this version of me for the one who never went through any of it. Not for a moment.

And I share all of this because I believe someone reading these words needed to hear it. Someone who is in the middle of something heavy right now. Someone who is carrying too much and doesn't know how to put it down. Someone who has been strong for so long that she's forgotten what it feels like to just be human. I want her to know: what you're walking through is not wasted. Even when it feels purposeless. Even when it feels like too much. Even when you can't see the shape of what's being built in you. It's happening. And the version of you waiting on the other side of this — she's worth every uncomfortable, uncertain, unpolished moment it takes to get there. Keep going. Not because everything is fine. But because you are being formed. And what's being formed in you is something only this process could produce.

And sometimes, that's the greatest clarity you can have.

Reflect & Respond

1. Looking back at a hard season, what do you see now that you couldn't see while you were in it?

2. What has the pressure produced in you that nothing else could have? What are you grateful for that you couldn't have been grateful for before?

3. What would you say to the woman you were at the beginning of your hardest season, if she could hear you now?

Chapter 20

Pressed... But Not Destroyed

There were moments I thought I wasn't going to make it through. Not in a way anyone else could see. Not in a way that showed up on the outside. But internally, there were moments I felt like I was being pressed on every side. Pressed by expectations. Pressed by responsibility. Pressed by the weight of everything I was carrying. And for a long time, I didn't know how much pressure I was under. Because I had learned how to function in it. How to move through it. How to carry it without letting it show. And when you've been doing that long enough, you start to believe you can handle anything. That you can keep going no matter what. That you won't break.

But the truth is, I did reach a breaking point. Not in a way that destroyed me. But in a way that stopped me. In a way that forced me to see what I had been ignoring. Because sometimes pressure reveals what strength has been hiding. It exposes what you've been carrying. It brings to the surface what you've been pushing down. And that's what it did for me. It showed me that I wasn't just strong — I was overwhelmed. It showed me that I wasn't just dependable — I was overextended. It showed me that I wasn't just handling everything — I was carrying things that were never mine.

And once I saw that, I couldn't unsee it. I couldn't go back to functioning the same way. So something had to change. And it did. Not overnight. Not all at once. But step by step. Decision by decision. Moment by moment. I started letting go. Of what I didn't need to carry. Of expectations that didn't belong to me. Of the version of myself that believed strength meant holding everything together. And in that process, I found something I didn't realize I had lost: myself. Not the version shaped by pressure. Not the version shaped by expectations. But the real version. The one who could breathe. The one who could rest. The one who didn't have to prove anything. And that version? She wasn't weak. She was whole.

Because I learned something through all of this: being pressed doesn't mean you're being destroyed. It means something is being revealed. Refined. Strengthened. Because pressure doesn't break what's built to last. It exposes what isn't meant to remain and strengthens what is. And I think of 2 Corinthians 4:8 — "We are hard pressed on every side, but not crushed; perplexed, but not in despair." I had read that verse countless times. But I never felt it the way I felt it in this season. Because Paul wasn't writing theory. He was writing from experience. And that verse became mine in a new way. Not as a motivational phrase. But as a testimony. Because I had lived it. I had been pressed. And I was still here. Not crushed. Not in despair. Changed. But here. And here is enough.

I also understand something now that I didn't then: everything I went through had purpose. Not because it felt good. Not because it was easy. But because it was necessary. It forced me to see. To slow down. To confront things I had been avoiding. To grow in ways I wouldn't have chosen on my own. And I want to say something to anyone who is currently in the building process, because it doesn't always look like building while it's happening. It looks like confusion. It looks like setbacks. It looks like things falling away that you thought were permanent. Building rarely announces itself as building while it's underway.

It usually only reveals itself in retrospect. Which is why you have to trust the process before you can see the product.

And through all of this, I learned something about strength. Because I spent so much of this journey redefining it. The world told me strength was how much I could carry. My own patterns told me strength was never letting anyone see me struggle. And both of those definitions nearly emptied me. But here is what I know now: true strength is the courage to be honest. It's the willingness to stop when everything says keep going. It's the humility to receive help, rest, and grace without earning it first. It's the faith to trust God in the silence. And it's the love for yourself that says: I am worth protecting. I am worth honoring. I am worth becoming. That is strength. And it was available to me all along. I just had to be willing to redefine it.

Pressed. But not destroyed. And if there's anything I want you to understand from this, it's this: whatever you're carrying right now, whatever feels heavy, whatever feels like it's pressing in on you from every side — it's not the end of you. It's the beginning of something deeper. Something stronger. Something more aligned than what you've been living. But you have to be willing to see it. To release what's not yours. To stop performing. To be honest about where you are. And to trust that what's being built in you is worth the process. Because it is. It always is.

And one day, you'll look back and realize the same thing I did: you weren't being broken. You were being built.

There was a time I thought letting go would feel like losing something. Like I would be left with empty spaces, with questions, with parts of me missing. But that's not what happened. What I released didn't take me with it. It revealed me.

And when everything that no longer belonged to me finally fell away, I wasn't left broken. I wasn't left searching. I was left with something I hadn't fully recognized before. A version of me that felt steady. Clear. At peace in a way that didn't need to be explained. Not because everything around me had changed. But because something within me had settled.

That's where this next part of my journey begins. Not in the breaking. Not in the healing. But in what came after.

Reflect & Respond

1. What does being pressed but not destroyed mean in your own story? Where have you felt the most pressure — and survived it?

2. How has your definition of strength changed? What did you used to believe strength looked like, and what do you know now?

3. What are you being built into? Even if you can't see it fully, what glimpses have you caught of who you are becoming?

Part Five

The Victory

Chapter 21

Walking in Wholeness

There was a time when I thought healing would feel like fireworks. Like something loud. Obvious. Undeniable. I thought I would wake up one day and just know — I'm healed now. Like it would be a moment I could point to. A day I could name. A clear before and after. But that's not how it happened. It didn't come with an announcement. No single obvious moment. No sudden shift where everything in my life magically aligned. It came quietly. So quietly that at first, I almost missed it.

Wholeness didn't arrive as a feeling. It showed up as a pattern. I noticed it in the way I responded to things that used to shake me. Situations that would have once sent me into overthinking, overexplaining, or overextending now barely moved me. And at first, I questioned it. Why doesn't this bother me anymore? Why don't I feel the need to react? Why am I okay? Not because I didn't care, but because I wasn't fragile anymore. There was a steadiness in me that I didn't recognize at first. A calm that didn't have to be forced. A groundedness that didn't depend on what was happening around me. A knowing that didn't require confirmation.

And wholeness, I discovered, isn't just something you feel in your mind or your spirit. It shows up in your body. I stopped waking up tense before the day even started. My jaw unclenched. My shoulders dropped. I stopped holding my breath the way I had been — that shallow, constant bracing for whatever came next. I started sleeping differently. Not just longer, but deeper. Like something that had been standing guard inside me finally sat down. My body was finally catching up to what my spirit had already started to receive. And that physical peace — that bodily rest — was something I hadn't even known I was missing until I finally had it.

And I want to be clear about what wholeness is not. Because I think we sometimes chase a version of it that doesn't exist. Wholeness is not the absence of hard days. It's not immunity from pain or disappointment or uncertainty. It's not a state where nothing can touch you or move you or challenge you. I still have hard days. I still feel things deeply. I still encounter moments that require me to choose intentionally. The difference is that those moments no longer destabilize me the way they used to. I can be moved without being swept away. I can feel without losing myself. I can face something difficult without it becoming an identity. That's not invincibility. That's wholeness. And it's a much more honest — and sustainable — thing to build toward.

I used to carry so many versions of myself. The one who tried to keep the peace. The one who stayed too long. The one who explained too much. The one who dimmed her voice just to be understood. And for a while, I thought healing meant fixing all of them. But what I've learned is this: I didn't need to fix her. I needed to release who I had to be to survive. Because she wasn't broken. She was responding to what she didn't yet know how to walk away from. And once I learned, I no longer needed to be her. Wholeness, for me, wasn't about becoming someone new. It was about no longer abandoning myself. That's the difference.

I've learned that wholeness doesn't mean everything in your life is perfect. It means you're no longer at war with yourself. And that war was exhausting. Constantly questioning myself. Second-guessing my decisions. Doubting what I felt. Overriding what I knew. Living disconnected from myself while trying to stay connected to everything else. But now that internal noise has quieted. There were parts of me I used to hide. The emotional parts. The uncertain parts. The parts that didn't have it all together. I thought those parts made me weak. But now I see it differently. Those were the parts that needed the most care. The most patience. The most grace. And instead of silencing them, I finally started listening. And in doing that, I became safer for myself.

There's a difference between being healed and being whole. Healing is the process. Wholeness is the posture. Healing says: I'm working through it. Wholeness says: I'm no longer defined by it. And I'm learning to stand in that. I no longer feel the need to revisit everything that hurt me. Not because it didn't matter, but because it no longer has control over me. I've made peace with things I once needed answers for. And that peace didn't come from understanding everything. It came from accepting what was and choosing not to carry it forward.

And I noticed how wholeness changed the way I showed up in relationships too. I stopped needing people to show up perfectly in order for me to feel secure. I stopped over-giving to fill a void I was responsible for filling myself. I stopped making myself smaller to make others more comfortable. And I stopped accepting less than I deserved and calling it grace. That's not grace. That's self-abandonment with a spiritual name. When you're whole, you can love generously without losing yourself. You can give freely without emptying yourself. And the relationships that are meant for the whole version of you will rise to meet her. The ones that only worked when you were depleted will naturally fall away. And that's not loss. That's alignment.

And maybe the biggest shift of all: I'm no longer chasing the version of me I thought I had to become. I'm embracing the woman I've grown into. She's not perfect. But she's honest. She's not always strong. But she's steady. She doesn't have all the answers. But she trusts her steps. She doesn't rush the process. She respects it. And for the first time, that feels like enough.

I wake up and I live. I move. I choose. I trust. I wake up and walk as her. Whole.

Reflect & Respond

1. What does wholeness feel like in your body, not just your mind or spirit? Where do you carry tension, and where are you beginning to release it?

2. How has becoming whole changed the way you show up in your relationships? What is different about the way you give now?

3. What does it mean to no longer be at war with yourself? What areas of internal conflict are you still working toward peace in?

Chapter 22

The Life I Once Prayed For

It didn't happen during a big moment. Not during celebration. Not when everything felt perfect. It happened on an ordinary day. The kind of day I would have once rushed through. I was moving through my routine, doing what I normally do, and something in me paused. Not physically. Internally. Like my spirit gently whispered: look. And when I did, I saw something I hadn't been paying attention to. Nothing around me had visibly shifted in that moment. But something in me recognized what had already changed. And it hit me. This life, this peace, this version of me — I had prayed for this.

Not casually. Not in passing. I'm talking about the kind of prayers that come from deep places. The kind you pray when you're tired of carrying everything alone. The kind you whisper when you don't even have the strength to speak loudly. The kind you cry when words don't come, but your heart still needs release. There was a version of me who asked God for this kind of peace. There was a version of me who just wanted to feel okay again. And now, here I was. Sitting in what I once only knew how to pray for.

And what made that moment so tender was remembering how desperate some of those prayers were. There were nights I didn't even have full sentences. Just a feeling. A groan. A leaning into God with nothing polished to offer. There were moments in the car, in the shower, in the quiet of a room I couldn't sleep in, where I just kept saying: please. Not with specific words. Not with a clear ask. Just: please. Help me. Meet me here. Change something. And I had almost forgotten those prayers. Not because they didn't matter, but because I had moved so far past the pain that prompted them. But standing in that ordinary moment, they came back to me. And I realized: He heard every single one.

And the truth is, I almost overlooked it. Because it didn't come the way I imagined. I thought the answer would look bigger. More obvious. More undeniable. But that's not how it came. It came quietly. Just like my healing did. It showed up in the small things. In the way I no longer wake up with heaviness on my chest. In the way my thoughts don't spiral the way they used to. In the way I can sit still without needing to escape myself. It showed up in what wasn't there anymore.

I used to think peace meant something was missing. Now I understand: peace means nothing is out of place.

There was a time when I prayed for clarity. And now I have it. Not because I know everything, but because I'm no longer confused about who I am. There was a time when I prayed for strength. And now I see it. Not in how much I can carry, but in what I no longer feel the need to hold onto. There was a time when I prayed to feel like myself again. And now I don't just feel like myself. I feel like a version of me I hadn't even met yet. A version of me that isn't defined by what she went through. A version of me that isn't searching for herself anymore. She's here.

And I want to say something about the gratitude that comes on the other side of survival. Because it's a specific kind of gratitude. It's not the gratitude of someone who got lucky. It's the gratitude of someone who can trace the hand of God through the hardest chapters and see — not just that He was there — but that He was working. That the silence was shaping something. That the waiting was building something. That the breaking was clearing the way for something truer. That kind of gratitude doesn't feel like performance. It feels like witness. Like you saw something happen and you can't help but say: I know what I know. And what I know is that I didn't get here alone.

I used to pray for this version of me. The one who doesn't settle. The one who doesn't shrink. The one who doesn't ignore her own voice. And now I see her. Not as a goal. But as my reality. And that has changed how I pray now. I don't just ask anymore. I acknowledge. I thank. I recognize. Because answered prayers don't always come wrapped in obvious outcomes. Sometimes they show up as peace you didn't have before. Strength you didn't realize you built. Clarity that quietly replaced confusion. And if you're not paying attention, you'll keep asking for what you've already received.

And I want to speak directly to the woman who is still in the waiting. The one who is still praying for what I'm now standing in. The one for whom the peace hasn't arrived yet. I see you. And I want you to know — your prayers are not falling on deaf ears. They are being heard. And the answer may not look the way you expect it to. It may not arrive when you think it should. But it is coming. And when it does, you may almost miss it — because it will likely come quietly, on an ordinary day, when you're not looking for it. That's how grace tends to move. Not with fanfare. But with a whisper that says: look. Look at what I've already done.

So now, I pause more. I reflect more. I sit in moments instead of rushing through them. Because this life, this peace, this version of me — she didn't just happen. She was prayed for. Cried for. Fought for. Grown into. And I honor her now. By not overlooking her. By not rushing past her. By not minimizing what it took to become her.

This is the life I once prayed for. And for the first time, I'm not just living it. I'm aware of it.

Reflect & Respond

1. When you look at your life right now, what prayers have already been answered that you may be overlooking?

2. What did you once desperately pray for that you now live in — even quietly, even imperfectly?

3. How has gratitude shifted for you from the other side of survival? What are you noticing that you would have rushed past before?

Chapter 23

Boundaries Became My Protection

There was a time when I thought boundaries were about keeping people out. It felt harsh. Uncomfortable. Almost wrong. I used to associate boundaries with distance. With disconnection. With becoming someone I didn't want to be. Part of why it felt so wrong was because of what I had been taught — directly and indirectly — about what it meant to be a good woman. Good women were accommodating. Good women made room. Good women didn't make things difficult or complicated. Good women showed up. And I internalized all of that. Not because it was said cruelly, but because it was modeled and celebrated. Flexibility was praised. Availability was rewarded. And so I became both, fully, without asking whether the cost was worth it. Nobody told me that accommodation without limits would eventually become a kind of self-erasure. And by the time I figured it out, I had already been practicing it for years.

And while grace is beautiful, misplaced grace will cost you. It cost me my peace. My clarity. My energy. There were moments when I felt drained and didn't even know why. Until I realized it wasn't everything around me. It was what I was allowing. That realization didn't come easy. Because it required me to take responsibility. Not for what people did, but for what I continued to tolerate. That question changed everything. It shifted me from frustration to awareness. From blame to accountability. And that's where boundaries started to take shape. Not from anger. Not from bitterness. But from clarity.

I started paying attention to what felt right and what didn't. To what drained me and what didn't. And instead of ignoring those things, I started honoring them. At first, it felt uncomfortable. Saying no felt unnatural. Choosing myself felt unfamiliar. But I had to learn this: just because something feels uncomfortable doesn't mean it's wrong. Sometimes it just means it's new. I had spent so much time being who others needed me to be that being who I needed to be felt foreign. But I didn't stop.

And there's a specific feeling I've learned to recognize now — the feeling that comes after you hold a boundary and it was the right call. It's not loud. It's not triumphant. It's quiet. It's a settling. Like something that had been slightly off-balance just found its footing. Your body knows before your mind catches up. That exhale you didn't realize you were holding. That release in your shoulders. That clarity that follows. I've learned to pay attention to that feeling. Because it's not guilt. Guilt is heavy and restless. This is different. This is peace confirming: you made the right choice. And the more I practiced recognizing that feeling, the easier it became to trust my own discernment.

I no longer felt the need to explain every decision. I no longer felt obligated to overextend just to keep the peace. I no longer felt responsible for how people responded to my limits. Because I finally understood something that changed everything: my responsibility is to be honest. Not to be accepted. Sometimes, the people who benefited from your lack of boundaries are the ones who struggle the most when you create them. And that can feel uncomfortable. It can make you question yourself. But I had to remind myself: I'm not becoming distant. I'm becoming disciplined with my peace. There's a difference.

Boundaries didn't make me cold. They made me clear. They didn't make me distant. They made me whole. They didn't push the right people away. They revealed who was aligned with me and who wasn't. And for the first time, I don't feel guilty about that. Because I understand now: not everyone is meant to have the same level of access to you. And that's not rejection. That's wisdom.

And I want to say something about boundaries in the context of faith. Because in some spiritual spaces, boundaries can be misread as unforgiveness, or pride, or a lack of love. But I've come to understand that wisdom and love are not opposites. Jesus himself withdrew from crowds. He said no to certain requests. He didn't heal every person in every city. He moved with intention. He protected his inner circle. He spent time alone to refuel. And if the Son of God practiced what looked like boundaries, then I can release the guilt of doing the same. Loving people well doesn't mean making yourself endlessly available to everyone at all times. Sometimes the most loving thing you can do — for yourself and for others — is to be honest about what you can and cannot carry. That's not a failure of love. That's love operating with wisdom.

So I no longer give from a place of pressure. I give from a place of overflow. I no longer stay where I feel misaligned. I move where I feel at peace. I no longer sacrifice myself to maintain connections. I choose connections that don't require me to.

Boundaries didn't limit my life. They protected it. And now, I move accordingly.

Reflect & Respond

1. Where in your life are boundaries protecting your peace right now? Where do you still need to build them?

2. How do you respond internally when you hold a boundary and it feels right? How is that different from guilt?

3. What does it mean to give from overflow rather than obligation? What needs to be in place for you to get there?

Chapter 24

I Don't Chase, I Align

There was a time when I believed if I wanted something bad enough, I had to go after it with everything in me. No pauses. No hesitation. No questions. Just movement. I thought that's what strength looked like. Going harder. Pushing more. Holding on tighter. And in some ways, that mindset did help me. It made me resilient. Focused. Determined. But what it didn't teach me was when to stop forcing things that weren't meant for me.

Because I wasn't just pursuing what was mine. I was chasing what felt familiar. What felt comfortable. What felt like something I needed to prove I could have. I chased clarity. I chased closure. I chased opportunities. I even chased people, in ways I didn't recognize at the time. Trying to make things make sense. Trying to make things work. Trying to make things stay. And the truth is, some of those things were never meant to stay.

And learning the difference between healthy pursuit and desperation took time. Because on the surface they can look the same — both involve effort, both involve showing up, both involve wanting something. But the internal experience is completely different. Healthy pursuit feels grounded. You want something and you move toward it, but you're not undone if it doesn't come. You're not adjusting your identity to receive it. Desperation, on the other hand, has an urgency to it. A grasping. A willingness to compromise things you shouldn't compromise just to hold on. I had operated from that desperation more than I wanted to admit. And recognizing it — calling it what it was — was the first step toward moving differently.

I've learned that alignment doesn't feel rushed. It doesn't feel confusing. It doesn't require you to question your worth or your place. Alignment feels steady. Clear. Natural. It flows. The effort doesn't feel like you're pulling something toward you. It feels like you're walking with something. And that shift changed everything. I no longer feel the need to chase what's meant for me. Because what's meant for me will meet me in my movement. Not in my desperation. Not in my overexertion. Not in my need to prove anything. Just in my alignment.

I don't need to force connections. I don't need to overextend to be seen. I don't need to convince anyone of my value. What aligns with me recognizes me. And what doesn't, I no longer try to adjust myself to fit it. I still move. I still pursue what matters to me. I still put in the work. But I move with discernment now. I pay attention to what feels right. To what flows. To what requires effort, but not strain. Because there's a difference. Effort builds. Strain depletes. And I've experienced both.

And that trust extended to God's timing in a way I hadn't experienced before. Because I used to approach timing as something to outrun. If I just moved fast enough, worked hard enough, I could make things happen on my timeline. But I've learned that God's timing doesn't bend to my urgency. And more importantly, I've learned that His timing is always better than mine. Things I thought I missed were actually things I was being protected from. Seasons I thought were delays were actually preparations. And the things that were truly mine — the things aligned with my purpose and my peace — they found me when I was ready. Not when I was desperate. When I was ready. And there's a profound rest in that.

So now, I move with intention. Not urgency. I make decisions from clarity. Not fear. I release what doesn't align without needing to hold onto it for understanding. Because I've learned something that brought me peace: everything doesn't need to make sense for me to let it go. That alone freed me. I no longer chase people who are unsure about me. I no longer chase opportunities that feel forced. I no longer chase outcomes that require me to abandon myself. Because what is aligned with me will not require me to become someone I'm not to receive it. And that truth has settled something deep within me.

So I don't chase anymore. I align. And I let what's meant for me find me in that alignment.

Reflect & Respond

1. Where in your life have you been chasing instead of aligning? What has that chasing cost you?

2. What does alignment feel like in your body and spirit, compared to forcing or straining toward something? Can you tell the difference?

3. What are you being called to trust God's timing on right now? What would it look like to move with intention rather than urgency?

Chapter 25

Becoming Her... For Real This Time

There was a time when I thought becoming her would look different than this. I thought it would feel louder. More noticeable. More complete. I thought I would arrive at some version of myself that had no questions. No moments of reflection. No reminders of what I had been through. But that's not what becoming her looks like.

Becoming her looks like standing in your life without needing to escape it. It looks like peace that doesn't need to be announced. Strength that doesn't need to be proven. Confidence that doesn't need validation. It looks like waking up and not feeling like you're chasing who you're supposed to be, because you're already walking as her.

And that realization didn't come overnight. It came through pressure. The kind of pressure that forces you to face yourself. The kind that stretches you beyond what feels comfortable. There were moments I didn't recognize myself. Moments I didn't like what I saw. Moments I wanted to go back to what felt familiar, even if it wasn't good for me. But I didn't go back. Not because I was always strong. But because something in me shifted.

And I want to be honest about what that shift required. Because it didn't just happen. It required me to stay in discomfort longer than felt natural. It required me to sit with uncertainty without immediately trying to resolve it. It required me to grieve some things — not just what I lost, but who I was when I was carrying too much. Because letting go of old patterns means letting go of an old self. And even when that old self was exhausted and overextended, she was familiar. And familiar has its own kind of comfort. Choosing the unfamiliar version of yourself — the whole one, the honest one, the one who doesn't perform — that takes courage. Quiet, daily, unannounced courage. And that's what becoming her actually looked like.

I stopped looking for comfort in places that cost me my peace. I stopped trying to rebuild versions of myself that I had already outgrown. I stopped negotiating with things I knew were no longer aligned. And that shift — that quiet, consistent shift — is what changed everything. Because growth isn't always loud. Sometimes it's the decisions you make in silence. The things you walk away from without announcing. The boundaries you hold without explaining. That's where I became her. Not in the big moments. But in the small ones. In the moments I chose peace over proving. In the moments I chose myself, without guilt.

She's softer now. But not weak. She's open. But not unguarded. She's grounded. Not shaken by everything that once moved her. She doesn't rush. She doesn't chase. She doesn't force. She trusts. And that trust didn't come from everything going right. It came from surviving what went wrong. It came from learning that even in the moments that felt like everything was falling apart, something was still being built.

And that's the part I understand now — the part I didn't see before. The pressure wasn't there to destroy me. It was there to refine me. To strip away what wasn't real. To expose what needed to heal. To shape me into someone I couldn't have become any other way. And now, when I look at my life, I don't see someone who avoided pressure. I see someone who walked through it and wasn't destroyed by it. I see someone who didn't lose herself — she found herself. She was shaped by it. Strengthened by it. Refined by it. And now she stands. Not hardened. Not closed off. But whole.

I'm not rushing to the next version of myself. I'm not trying to skip ahead. I'm not looking for something outside of me to complete me. Because I'm already here. And maybe that's what this entire journey was about. Not becoming someone different. But becoming someone real. Someone who can stand in her life without shrinking. Without performing. Without pretending. Just being. Fully. Honestly. Completely.

So this isn't just an ending. It's a recognition. Of everything I've walked through. Everything I've released. Everything I've grown into. And most importantly, everything I didn't let break me. Because the pressure came. But it didn't destroy me. It revealed me.

And to you — the one holding this book right now — I want you to know that this story is not just mine. The weight you've been carrying, the exhaustion you've been pushing through, the version of yourself you've been quietly losing — I see it. And I want you to know: you are not too far gone. You are not too tired. You are not too broken. You are exactly at the beginning of something. And the woman you are becoming — the one on the other side of your pressure, your surrender, your letting go — she is worth every uncomfortable step it takes to get there. Don't give up on her. Don't settle back into what was just because it's familiar. She's waiting for you. And she's everything you've been praying for.

And now I walk in that truth. Not as who I used to be. Not as who I thought I had to become. But as who I am. For real this time.

Reflect & Respond

1. Describe the woman you are becoming. Not who you used to be, not who you think you should be — who are you right now, for real?

2. What did it take to get here? Name the moments, the decisions, the quiet courage that brought you to this version of yourself.

3. What is one thing you want to carry forward from this book — one truth, one practice, one permission you are giving yourself?

A Prayer for the Woman Becoming

Heavenly Father,

I come before You humble as I know how not as someone who has it all together, but as someone who is still becoming. Asking You to forgive me for all my sins and transgressions.

Thank You for carrying me through the seasons I didn't understand. Thank You for the moments when I felt weak, overwhelmed, and unsure — and You never left me. Lord, You saw every silent battle. Every tear I didn't explain. Every weight I carried that no one else knew about. And still... You kept me.

You kept me when I was performing strength I didn't have. You kept me when my prayers were broken and unpolished. You kept me in the silence, when I couldn't feel You but needed You most. That keeping — I don't take it lightly. It is the evidence of a faithfulness I didn't always recognize, but can see clearly now.

Father, I release everything that was never mine to carry. The pressure. The expectations. The need to be everything for everyone. I lay it all at Your feet.

I lay down the identity I built around what I could carry. I lay down the fear of being seen as less if I carry less. I lay down the version of strength that was slowly draining me. And I receive, in its place, what You have always offered: rest for the weary, grace for the overwhelmed, and a yoke that is easy and a burden that is light.

Teach me how to walk in peace. Teach me how to trust You without needing all the answers. Teach me how to rest in who You created me to be. Strengthen me in the areas where I once felt weak. Restore the parts of me that felt lost. Renew my mind, my spirit, and my confidence in You.

Help me to set boundaries without guilt. To choose alignment over approval. To walk boldly in the identity, You've given me.

Lord, remind me daily — that I am not broken. I am not forgotten. I am not defeated. I am being rebuilt.

And I trust the Builder. I trust that You know what You're doing in me, even when I can't see it. Even when the process is uncomfortable. Even when what's being removed hurts more than I expected. I trust that what You are building in me is stronger, truer, and more aligned with Your purpose than anything I could have constructed on my own.

And everything I went through... is not the end of my story. It is the foundation of who I am becoming.

Thank You for being my strength when I had none left. Thank You for meeting me in my honesty. Thank You for showing me that surrender is not weakness — it is where You begin.

From this day forward, I choose to walk differently. With peace. With clarity. With faith. And no matter what comes, I will remember: *I was pressed... but not destroyed.*

In Jesus' name, Amen.

www.ingramcontent.com/pod-product-compliance
Lightning Source LLC
LaVergne TN
LVHW090530110826
845146LV00003B/1040